If I WeRe You

Words & Pictures by

Gary Turchin

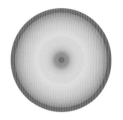

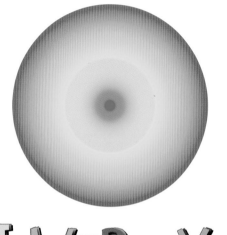

If I WeRe YoU

©2012 Gary Turchin
All rights reserved.
No part of this book may be reproduced in any way without permission.
Printed in China through Bolton Associates, Inc., San Rafael, CA

ISBN: 978-0-9646099-0-7
www.garyturchin.net
www.IfIWereYouthebook.com
garyturchin@gmail.com

To whom it may concern

Simon DeWitt & Friends

OAKLAND, CALIFORNIA

I tell myself...

Then I'd put my clothes on backwards just to make sure I wasn't going in the wrong direction in the first place.

If I WeRe YoU

I'd Smile with my eyes
and Listen with my kNows.

I'd eat oranges and avocados
play with friends,
laugh cry Sing SHOUT,
THINK on my feet,
and DANCE
on my toes...

...because If I WERE YOU, I'd be a human being with a **big,** **BEAUTIFUL,** **human heart** beating inside of me.

And there's **NOTHING** wrong with that.

If I WeRe YoU

I'd sit under a NECTARINE tree
in the August heat,
and I'd eat as many
NECTARINES as I could.
And if someone said,
   "You're going to get sick!"
      I'd say,
         "You gotta be crazy. No one
      gets sick of NECTARINES."

If I Were You

I wouldn't stray too far from the Sun.

But I wouldn't play too close to it, either.

An Earth's distance away

is just about right.

IF I WERE YOU

I'd find a **spot** somewhere on the Earth
and I'd call it "**My Spot**."
And I'd go sit on **My Spot** every once in a while,
and I'd listen to whatever it had to say
in whatever language it had to say it,
because **spots** know things only **spots** can know.
Then I'd say, "Thanks, **Spot.** You really hit the spot."

Spots

If I Were You

I wouldn't try to fix Dad's pocket watch,
the one that belonged to *his* Dad—
it hasn't worked in years.
And I wouldn't go near the little screws
in the back,
as tempting as they are,
because once I unscrewed them,
and turned the watch over...
there would be no going back
in time.

If I WERE YOU

I'd tell time by SUNDIAL.
The only moving part
is the SUN.
And at night,
it turns itself off
to save batteries.

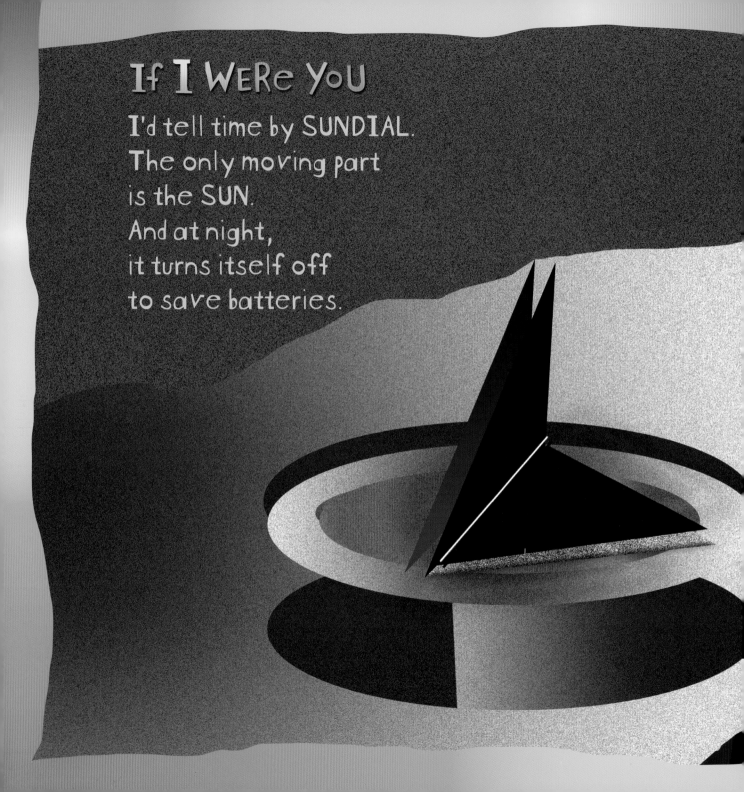

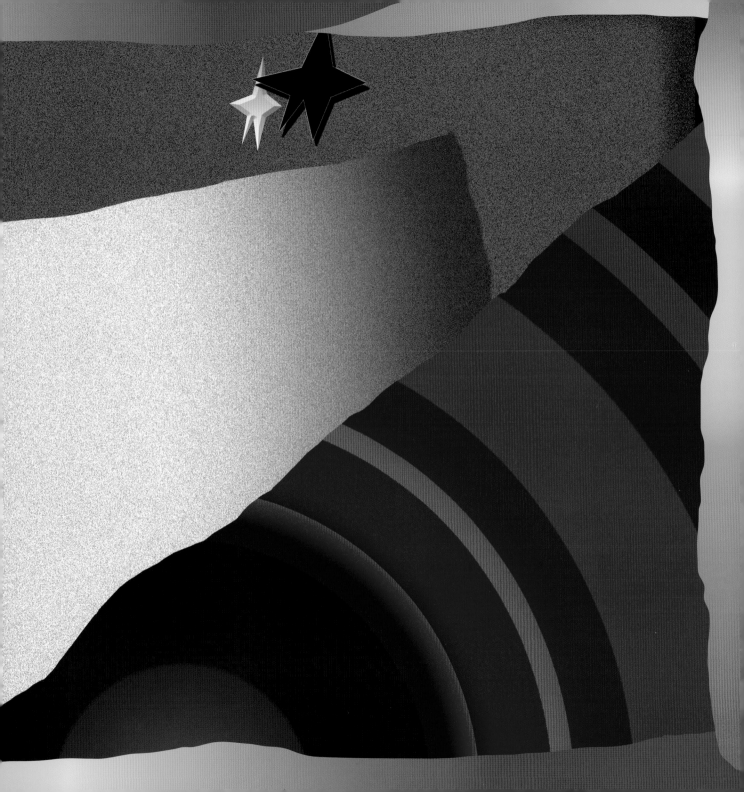

...and for SUNFLOWERS to spread like DANDELIONS, across soccer fields and golf courses, out of sidewalk cracks, next to parking meters and "No U-Turn"signs.
Everywhere you turn:
SUNFLOWERS!

If I WERE YOU
I'd believe in
CATS,
and Curiosity,
and NINE lives'
worth of
second chances
and do-overs...

If I WERe YOU

I'd invest in rainbows,
they'll always
be worth something
no matter who's in charge.

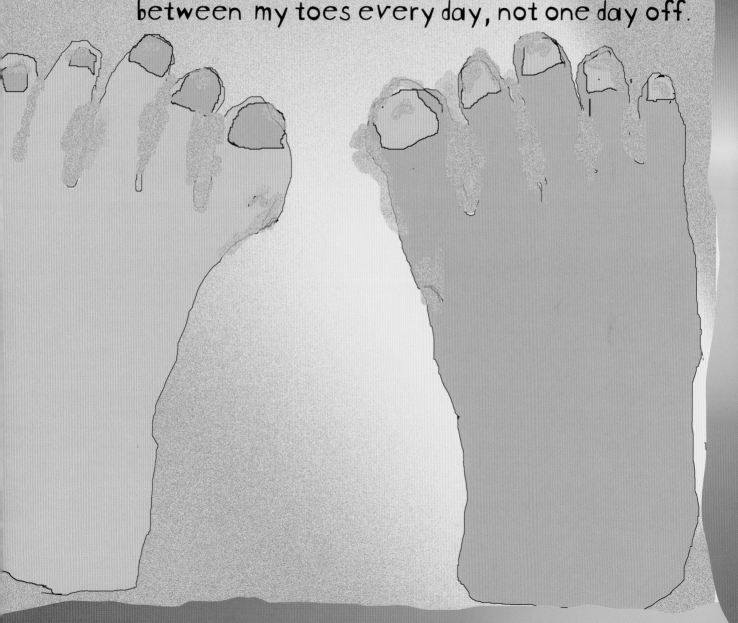

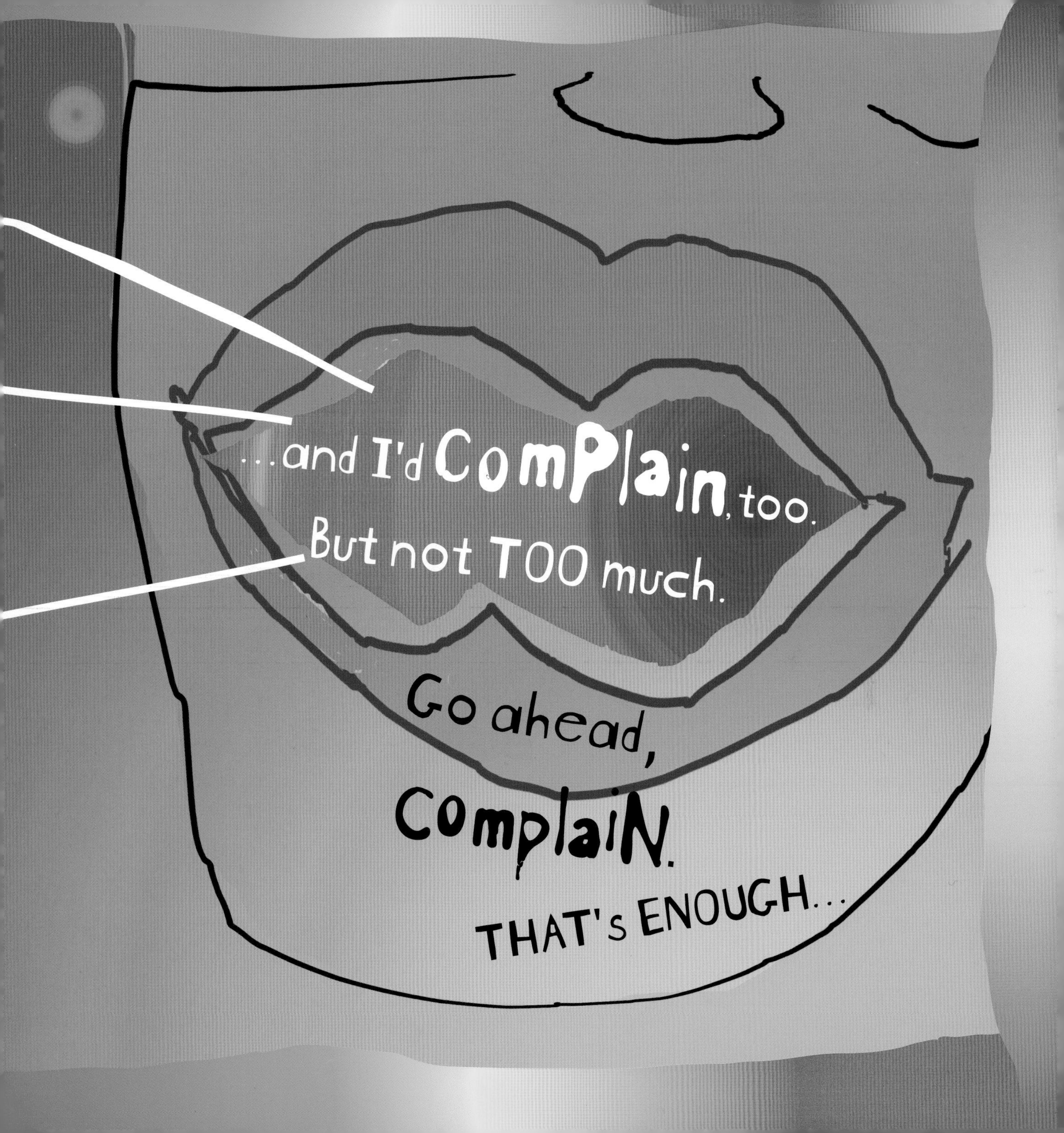
...and I'd ComPlain, too.
But not TOO much.
Go ahead,
Complain.
THAT's ENOUGH...

If **I** WeRe YoU
I'd root for the **HOME** TEAM

If we don't win,
it's more than a **SHAME.**

If I WERe YOU

I'd make friends with a giraffe.
They have the biggest hearts,
and that's all you need
to know about giraffes...

...or friends.

...and **I**'d invent something
that could save the world,
   If it ever needed
   saving.
And hopefully it won't,
   But if it did,
I'd let the world use
   my invention
FREE of **CHARGE**.

If I WERE YOU

I'd get a JOB that didn't feel like a JOB,

because doing it is all I ever wanted to do.

And if someone FULL of IMPORTANCE

were to stop and say,

"You know, eventually you'll have

to get a real job."

I'd say, "Well, you know,

– eventually you'll have to get a

REAL DREAM."

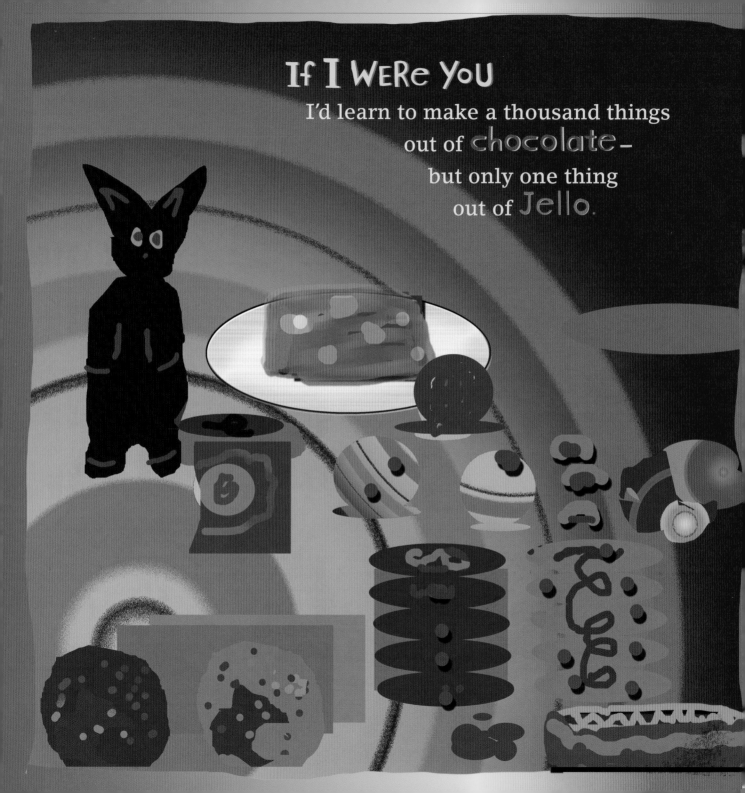

If I WERe YOU
I'd drop my leaves
every autumn,
because growing them back
is one of life's greatest
pleasures.

If I WeRe YoU
I'd quit *caterpillaring* around
and start butterflying.

If I WERe YOU

I'd believe in FOREVER,
And I'd thank my lucky stars
that FOREVER believed in me.

Thank you!

¡GRACIAS!

ARIGATô!

Mahalo!

Merci!

XIÉ XIE

SPASIBA!

ASANTE!

Thanks!

To be continued...

sweet dreams...

Special thanks to:
Deborah Green, for her keen artistic insight and support.
Also to Joanne at Bolton Printing, Tom Levy, Gene Fredericks, Linda Jay Geldens, Susan M. Davis,
Liz Wiener, My brother David, Lucy & Katy, Dr. Marcey & team, the SFWW, & my sangha.